YOU GOAL, GIRL

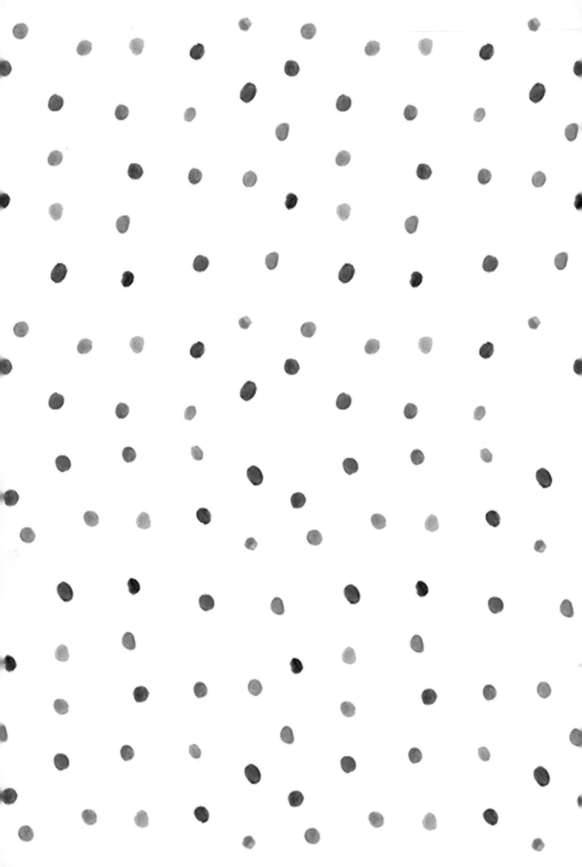

THE TOTALLY APPROACHABLE, NOT-SCARY GUIDES

YOU GOAL, GIRL

A GOAL-SETTING WORKBOOK

MELEAH BOWLES AND **ELISE WILLIAMS**

THE CREATORS OF *EARN SPEND LIVE*

ROCK
POINT

Inspiring | Educating | Creating | Entertaining

Brimming with creative inspiration, how-to projects, and useful information to enrich your everyday life, Quarto Knows is a favorite destination for those pursuing their interests and passions. Visit our site and dig deeper with our books into your area of interest: Quarto Creates, Quarto Cooks, Quarto Homes, Quarto Lives, Quarto Drives, Quarto Explores, Quarto Gifts, or Quarto Kids.

First published in 2018 by Rock Point,
an imprint of The Quarto Group
142 West 36th Street, 4th Floor
New York, NY 10018 USA
T (212) 779-4972 F (212) 779-6058
www.QuartoKnows.com

Illustrations by Jasmine Av
Designed by Katie Cooper

Rock Point titles are also available at discount for retail, wholesale, promotional, and bulk purchase. For details, contact the Special Sales Manager by email at specialsales@quarto.com or by mail at The Quarto Group, Attn: Special Sales Manager, 401 Second Avenue North, Suite 310, Minneapolis, MN 55401, USA.

10 9 8 7 6 5 4 3 2 1

ISBN: 978-1-63106-575-0

Editorial Director: Rage Kindelsperger
Managing Editor: Erin Canning
Editor: Keyla Hernández
Cover and Interior Design: Katie Cooper
Illustration Design: Jasmine Av
Design Manager: Phil Buchanan

Printed in China

DEDICATION

To Dana Robbins for believing in us, harassing us about our ten-year plans, and orchestrating this beautiful partnership.

—Elise and Meleah

CONTENTS

INTRODUCTION

f you're reading this, you're one of three people: 1) the type who lives by their daily or weekly planner and thrives on checking off their to-dos; 2) the type who breaks out into hives when their boss asks them about their ten-year plan; or 3) you're a mix of both; you love planning and making to-do lists, but you need some help sticking to plans and goals.

Regardless, you're in the right place. If you already love goal setting, you will have an absolute blast filling out these worksheets and taking your goals to the next level. If you're more of a goal-setting newbie, you'll be a total pro by the time we're done with you. In this workbook, we'll not only introduce you to goal setting, habit building, and other tactics to help you make your dreams a reality, but also walk you through everything step by step.

We are by no means productivity experts, and we've never pretended to be; we're just two typical twentysomethings faking it til' we make it, like you. In fact, the two of us are naturally (extremely) lazy Type Bs. (It's okay, so is Chrissy Teigen. She said/tweeted so herself: "Trying to think of someone more lazy than me but only coming up with the inanimate objects currently surrounding me.")

But laziness doesn't get you a promotion. It doesn't wash that mile-high stack of laundry. It doesn't help you get your butt to the gym. Since entering adulthood, we quickly learned that we'd have to adopt a few Type-A habits—like setting goals, actually completing to-do lists, and just generally getting things done—to succeed at anything.

We've also learned a lot about goal setting from the research we've done creating Earn Spend Live, the interviews we've conducted with planning and productivity experts, the more-than-fifty planners and productivity tools we've reviewed on the site, and all of the mistakes we've made along the way. (Plus, you'll find a few words of wisdom from psychologists and goal-setting experts sprinkled throughout this book; so you don't just have to take our word.)

Because you picked up this book and made it this far, we're assuming you have some goals you want to achieve—or you at least want help setting realistic, achievable goals.

And if your parents bought this for you, we're assuming their gift is a not-so-subtle hint that they want you to stop floating aimlessly through life and maximize your potential. (And remember to thank them later.)

Whether you're naturally Type A or Type B, this goal-setting workbook is for you. Whether you're a goal-setting pro or a beginner, this workbook is for you. Whether you're more of a short-term goal setter or a big-picture, ten-year-plan goal setter, this workbook is for you.

While there is a definite method to goal-setting madness, this workbook is 100% what you make it. The following worksheets are completely customizable, so take our instructions and then make the workbook pages work for you, your lifestyle, and your goals!

WHAT IS **EARN SPEND LIVE**?

In 2015, we created Earn Spend Live—a lifestyle website devoted to helping young women navigate their career, manage their finances, and figure out how to be an adult. At the time, we were navigating our first jobs post college and figuring everything out as we went—how to make a five-year plan, how to set goals we won't ditch in two days, and how to balance our time between work, adult responsibilities, and getting enough sleep at night (although we're still trying to figure that last one out).

As we stumbled along, we wished we had some kind of guide to help us understand how to focus the goals and decisions we were making—aside from the typical advice you find online for millennials, like if you just "hustle," become a "girlboss," and drink enough coffee, you too can achieve success. (Spoiler alert: There's a lot more to achieving success than that.)

So with a push from our mentor, who believes in us far too much, we decided to make our own guide—aka Earn Spend Live—where we detail our own successes (like getting a book deal in our mid-twenties) and mistakes (like taking on too much and inevitably metaphorically combusting), as well as share advice from women much more successful than us.

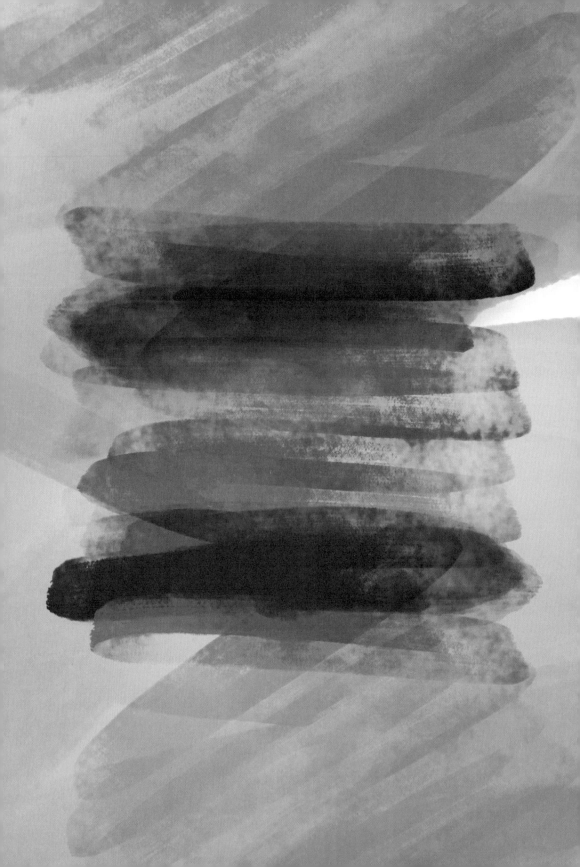

CHAPTER 1

GOAL SETTING 101

A goal is something you have some control over. Things you can control: your behavior. Things you cannot control: literally anything else. You're probably thinking, "what's the point?" The point is that although goal setting may seem like an abstract concept (at least to us Type Bs, anyway), there is a right way to set goals—and a wrong way.

If you've had trouble achieving goals in the past, it might be because you weren't actually setting real goals to begin with. Let's go over what goals are and what they aren't.

Basically, any goal that relies on other people or external factors in order to be achieved is not a good goal. Your goals are set by you, so you should be the controlling factor. You can't control when you'll meet the love of your life, but you can control the state of your finances so you'll be ready when that day comes.

Getting a promotion at work is your boss's decision (and your boss's boss), but you can put in the time and effort to get there by showing up, doing your best, documenting your achievements, and, of course, taking the incredibly important step to **ASK FOR IT.**

• •

NOT A GOAL:

X Getting married

X Having a baby

X Getting a promotion

GOAL:

✓ Saving money for a wedding

✓ Being financially ready to have/raise a baby

✓ Mastering a new skill

• •

You can also think of this as dreams vs. goals. It's perfectly fine to dream about living in a mansion, Kardashian-style. But how specifically are you going to get there? Goals are the steps you take to make your dreams a reality.

"Nothing is ever achieved in life without goal setting. Even the decision to get into your car, drive to the grocery store, and buy a gallon of milk requires setting a goal and following through. The reality is that our decisions and choices create our life day by day. We are already envisioning goals, deciding to create them, and making them happen."

—Dr. Susan Shumsky, best-selling author

Now that we're clear on what goals ARE, what about realistic goals vs. unrealistic goals?

UNREALISTIC GOALS:	REALISTIC GOALS:
X Writing a book in a week	✓ Writing 500 words per day
X Losing 30 pounds in 2 months	✓ Exercising 4 days a week
X Doubling my salary in a year	✓ Negotiating a raise this year

THE WRONG WAY TO SET GOALS

When you decide to start working on You 2.0 (which, for us, is a weekly thing), you have an idea in your head of what You 2.0 looks like. In our experience, the You 2.0 in our heads is basically Wonder Woman (including the demi-god strength, hand-eye coordination, and knowledge of seven languages). You will make every change you want to make, and you will do it immediately.

But realistically, if you set out to be Wonder Woman, you're going to fall short. Zeus didn't shape you from clay, and you probably weren't raised on an island full of women warriors.

In theory, setting high standards for yourself should still work out in your favor, right? It might. But you also might spread yourself too thin and only accomplish one, maybe two of your goals.

What happens when you don't achieve your goals time and time again? Well, first of all, it's not a very satisfying feeling. But more importantly, it can set up a certain expectation— that you won't ever meet your goals, which becomes a self-fulfilling prophecy—and then you won't believe in setting goals at all. It also has a negative effect on you emotionally. You don't meet your goals, and then you feel like you're a failure—which sucks, because you're not a failure. And WE believe in YOU!

THE RIGHT WAY TO SET GOALS

When you focus on only a few important goals, you're more likely to achieve them. You only have so much time in a day and so much energy in your body. The hard part, however, is actually limiting yourself to just a few of the most important, smart goals.

You've *likely* heard of S.M.A.R.T. goals* before, but if you haven't, or if you have but you need a refresher:

Specific
Measurable
Achievable
Realistic
Time-bound

*Although we wish we came up with this idea, S.M.A.R.T. goals has been discussed in many published works before us.

Example of a S.M.A.R.T. goal: I want to pay off $2,000 of credit card debt in the next four months; broken down, I'll make a payment of $250 per paycheck. $2,000 is the **specific** goal amount. I can **measure** how much I've paid each month. I've adjusted my budget and cut back on other expenses, so $500 per month is **achievable** and **realistic**. And I have a specific **timeline** to achieve my goal.

S.M.A.R.T. goals work because they're quantifiable, which means you can measure your success. If your goal is just "reading more books," how can you measure that? Reading more books compared to what, exactly? Instead, count up how many books you read last year, decide how many more you want to read this year, and decide on a specific number of books you want to read. Then decide your timeline—do you want to read twenty-five books this year, or two books per month?

BRAIN DUMP

The first step toward setting S.M.A.R.T. goals? Writing them down. You're 42% more likely to achieve your goals when you write them down, according to a study conducted by

Dr. Gail Matthews, a psychology professor at the Dominican University in California. So get comfy, get cozy, and then do a goals brain dump.

The key to a solid brain dump is to write down whatever comes to your mind without judging it. Even if you know it's not a fully formed S.M.A.R.T. goal, or even the most realistic goal right now, write it down anyway. The brain dump is a safe space. You can re-evaluate and prioritize after everything is on paper.

For example, if your initial goal is something broad, like "lose weight," that's perfectly fine for now; write it down in your brain dump. Then later, with the help of the following worksheets, you can refine that goal to be "lose ten pounds," and your steps to achieve said goal could be "cook more meals at home, drink X oz of water each day, and exercise four days a week." But we'll get to that later.

It should be noted that we don't think you need to lose weight; you're perfect the way you are. But losing weight is a common goal, so we'll use that example a few times throughout this book.

INSTRUCTIONS: Use this space to brainstorm some goals.

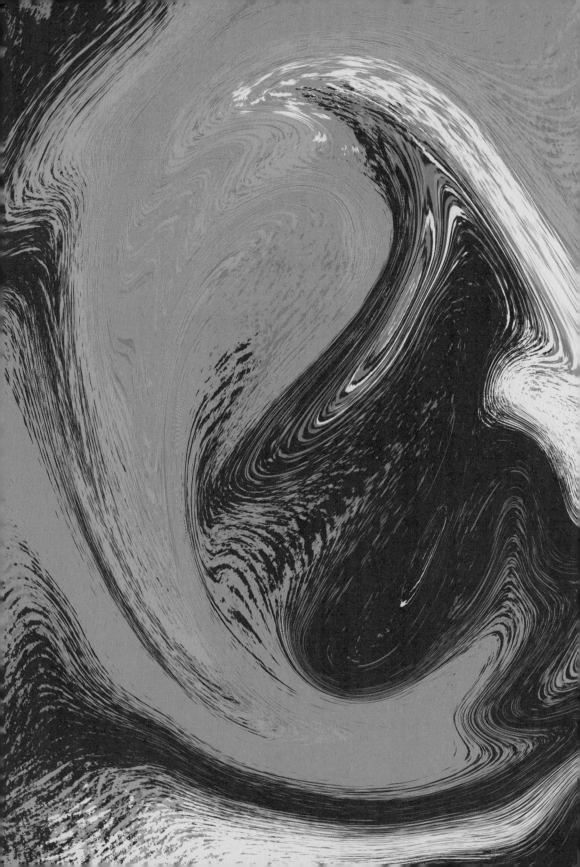

CHAPTER 2

PRIORITIZING YOUR GOALS

nfortunately, unlike our girl Diana Prince*, we're humans, with regular human DNA. That means we can't actually accomplish every single thing we set out to do, no matter how hard we try; so not every goal you write down on your Brain Dump will make it to your Top Goals, no matter how S.M.A.R.T. it may be.

But for now, sort all of them into the following five main categories:

Professional Development

Personal Development

Health + Fitness

Hobbies

Finances

*Wonder Woman's alias.

Once you have everything sorted, take a good, hard look at the goals laid out in front of you.

Consider the following:

• **Which goals would be the easiest to achieve?**

• **Which goals are most important to me?**

• **Which goals will improve my life the most?**

• **Which goals are realistic?**

It's important to note that while we can give you questions to consider to narrow down your goals, we can't actually tell you which goals to choose. It's your life, and you know how to best improve it. So use your critical-thinking skills, grab a highlighter, and highlight your top goal in each category. If you happen to have two highlighters handy, you can also choose a runner-up goal in each category too.

If you don't have goals for all five areas, that's fine. The important thing is that you have goals that are important and meaningful to you. If you have four different financial goals you're hoping to accomplish, then maybe that's all you focus on for a year.

PRO TIP: ·

Work-life balance is a myth, and not everyone is good at multitasking; it's perfectly fine to focus on making improvements in just one (or two) of these categories at a time!

· ·

You know yourself better than anyone, so it's up to you to set your limits so you don't spread yourself too thin. You can realistically probably only really be good at a couple of these things at a time, so don't feel like you have to achieve everything at once in order to be "successful."

Choose a couple of these categories to focus on for now if you want, and then go from there! Or choose a goal from each category. You do you.

Finances

INSTRUCTIONS:

Sort the goals from your

brain dump (pages 20-21)

into these five categories.

Hobbies

Professional Development

Personal Development

Health + Fitness

SORT IT OUT

1.

CATEGORY:

....

2.

CATEGORY:

....

3.

CATEGORY:

....

4.

CATEGORY:

....

INSTRUCTIONS:

Write down your top five goals and corresponding categories.

5.

CATEGORY:

....

CHAPTER 3

ACHIEVING YOUR GOALS

ow that you've chosen your top five goals, it's time to lay the groundwork for actually achieving them. It's not enough to just set a goal and call it a day; you have to set minigoals (aka actionable steps) and figure out how to best achieve each goal step by step.

Thinking through each goal and seeing the big picture can be difficult, so we've laid out a few questions for you to answer for each of your top goals.

Why do I want to achieve this goal? How will it better my life?
First things first, you have to know your WHY. Why do you want to learn a new skill, save up a certain amount, or break a bad habit? How will this improve your life?

The more important the end result is to you, the more likely you are to work your butt off to achieve your goal.

What's the timeline for this goal? When is my deadline?
You're more likely to finish a task quickly if your boss gives you a deadline, right? So why should the goals you set for yourself be any different? Figure out how long it would realistically take you to achieve your goal, and then set a deadline for yourself.

Who will help me stay on-track with this goal? How will they hold me accountable?
Rome wasn't built in a day, and it certainly wasn't built by one single Roman. While the goals you set should be 100% about Y.O.U., as we've said twenty billion times by now, the truth is everything is easier with a support system holding you accountable for your actions.

You're more likely to actually go to the gym if you have a workout buddy, you're more likely to stick to your no-spending challenge if you tell people about it, and writing two books in one year is a lot more doable if you have a coauthor (wonder how we know that?). All this is to say that when you're coming up with specific steps to achieve your goals, consider who will help you along the way. And remember to thank the little people later.

"Talking to a trusted friend, therapist, or mentor about your goal puts it out into the Universe, making it more real. They can follow up with you, help you strategize if you get stuck, and celebrate your successes with you."

—**Bianca L. Rodriguez, MA, Ed.M, LMFT**

What tools do I need to be able to achieve this goal?

If your goal is to lose weight, you'll probably want to sign up for a gym membership or invest in some home equipment. If you want to learn how to budget, build up an emergency fund, or pay off your debts, you could use our budgeting workbook, *Common Cents*, as a guide.

What three actionable steps will I take to achieve this goal? ICYMI*, a goal without a specific plan behind it is useless. Break down your goal into three actionable steps.

Example: My goal is to save up $500 for a new camera. My steps would be:

1. Evaluate my budget and cut spending from at least two areas.

2. Sit down and do the math to figure out how much I need to save per paycheck and how often.

3. Set up an auto-draft to automatically move a set amount of money from one account to another on a set day each month (or however often you want the money to be transferred—it's pretty much the best invention ever).

What steps will I take each week to achieve this goal?
Take your actionable steps and break them down weekly. If this is a monetary goal, it could be saving a certain amount

*ICYMI means In Case You Missed It. We don't know how long people are still going to be saying it, in case you're reading this a decade after we wrote it.

each week. If it's a fitness goal, it could be taking a fitness class each week. Basically, how can you measure your progress each week?

What steps will I take each day to achieve this goal?
Now break them down into daily habits, if possible. If it's a monetary goal, this could be something like cutting back on daily expenses, i.e. taking your lunch to work instead of dining out—so the daily habit would be packing your lunch every night. If it's a fitness goal, it could be drinking a certain amount of water each day or walking a certain number of steps. (We'll delve more into forming habits and how they help you achieve your goals in Chapter 5.)

How will I reward myself once this goal is achieved?
If there's a light at the end of the tunnel (like fro-yo, or a road trip with your friends), you're much more likely to stay positive and put in the work to achieve your goals. Treat yo' self. But make sure you're treating yourself in accordance with the goal. If your goal is to build your emergency fund, then your reward shouldn't be a new, pricey television.

GOAL #1

Goal: ....

Why do I want to achieve this goal? How will it better my life? ....

....

....

....

What's my timeline for this goal? When is my deadline? ....

....

....

....

Who will help me stay on-track with this goal? How will they hold me accountable

....

....

....

What tools do I need to achieve this goal?.................................

....

....

....

tegory: ....

hat three actionable steps will I take to achieve this goal?

....

....

....

hat steps will I take each week to achieve this goal?.................

....

....

....

hat steps will I take each day to achieve this goal? ....

....

....

....

ow will I reward myself once this goal is achieved?.....................

....

....

....

GOAL BREAKDOWN

GOAL #2

Goal: ....

Why do I want to achieve this goal? How will it better my life? ....

....

....

....

What's my timeline for this goal? When is my deadline? ....

....

....

....

Who will help me stay on-track with this goal? How will they hold me accountable

....

....

....

What tools do I need to achieve this goal? ....

....

....

....

tegory: ....

hat three actionable steps will I take to achieve this goal?

....

....

....

hat steps will I take each week to achieve this goal? ....

....

....

....

hat steps will I take each day to achieve this goal? ....

....

....

....

w will I reward myself once this goal is achieved? ....

....

....

....

GOAL BREAKDOWN

GOAL #3

Goal: ....

Why do I want to achieve this goal? How will it better my life? ....

....

....

....

What's my timeline for this goal? When is my deadline? ....

....

....

....

Who will help me stay on-track with this goal? How will they hold me accountable

....

....

....

What tools do I need to achieve this goal?...

....

....

....

tegory: ....

at three actionable steps will I take to achieve this goal?

....

....

....

at steps will I take each week to achieve this goal?...................

....

....

....

at steps will I take each day to achieve this goal? ....

....

....

....

w will I reward myself once this goal is achieved?.....................

....

....

....

GOAL BREAKDOWN

 **GOAL #4**   Goal: ....

Why do I want to achieve this goal? How will it better my life? ....

....

....

....

What's my timeline for this goal? When is my deadline? ....

....

....

....

Who will help me stay on-track with this goal? How will they hold me accountable

....

....

....

What tools do I need to achieve this goal? ....

....

....

....

tegory: ....

at three actionable steps will I take to achieve this goal?

....

....

....

at steps will I take each week to achieve this goal?..................

....

....

....

at steps will I take each day to achieve this goal? ....

....

....

....

w will I reward myself once this goal is achieved?......................

....

....

....

GOAL BREAKDOWN

GOAL #5

Goal: ....

Why do I want to achieve this goal? How will it better my life? ....

....

....

....

What's my timeline for this goal? When is my deadline? ....

....

....

....

Who will help me stay on-track with this goal? How will they hold me accountable

....

....

....

What tools do I need to achieve this goal? ....

....

....

....

tegory: ....

at three actionable steps will I take to achieve this goal?

....

....

....

at steps will I take each week to achieve this goal? ....

....

....

....

at steps will I take each day to achieve this goal? ....

....

....

....

w will I reward myself once this goal is achieved? ....

....

....

....

GOAL BREAKDOWN

PRO TIP:

Take a Creative Break.

If you start to feel overwhelmed by all the goal setting in this book, find a notebook and take a little doodling break. If you don't like doodling, give a coloring break a shot. Because like earning a paycheck, doing your laundry, budgeting, or literally any "adult" thing, setting goals is essential ... but not always fun (you did read the part where we say we're really, truly lazy, right?).

Reason #1: Creativity is awesome.

Reason #2 (and maybe a better reason: Being creative helps you relax. As early as the 1900s, psychologist Carl G. Jüng found that coloring is a powerful relaxation technique. That means coloring is a great way to take a break if you're feeling overwhelmed from all of the goal-setting. Bonus: When you're relaxed, it's easier to focus on your goals. (And we can 100% vouch; coloring and doodling really helped us focus on our goal of meeting deadlines for this book!)

If you're not into reasons from the 20th century, here's one for the modern day from Zainy Pirbhai, MFT who specializes in art therapy:

"Adult coloring can be very therapeutic and relaxing. It can be compared to a form of meditation, because it's helping unplug from life and focusing on a task in the present. Coloring can help your brain zone out and decrease negative thoughts. It has also been known to reduce stress and anxiety."

Reason #3: Being creative gives you endorphins; endorphins make you happy; and happy people just don't abandon their goals! (We embellished here a little, but you get the point.)

CHAPTER 4

GRATITUDE LOG

t's easy to feel happy and positive when you're making real progress on your goals. But life isn't a straight, upward trajectory; there are inevitably going to be some a lot of setbacks.

One way to stay on the sunny side is to take a breather and make a point to think of (at least) one thing that's going right each day. Some days all you will be able to think of is something as simple and ordinary as enjoying your morning cup of coffee or reading a good book, but if you look hard enough, there are always little sprinkles of happiness throughout even the toughest days.

Maintaining a feeling of gratitude is good for your health, too! Practicing gratitude can help you keep your cool and feel more patient, improve your sleep, and support feelings of happiness.

Strive to make gratitude a consistent habit. By taking just one minute a day and jotting down something you're grateful for, you can train your brain to focus more on the good things that are happening all around you.

"When we are stuck in a negative spiral, gratitude allows us to steer our attention away from the depression, stress, and anxiety and focus on the gratitude, joy, and peace. While our circumstances may not change, our experiences of those circumstances may start to feel different. Gratitude is a muscle. The more we exercise it, the easier it becomes to stay in a positive mind state."

—Musa Francis, Radical Self-Care Coach

Tracking what makes you happy can also help you to identify new goals to set. If trying out a new recipe makes you happy, set a goal to take a cooking class or try new recipes once a week. If being recognized for your achievements at work is what you're grateful for, set goals around professional development. If the only thing you can come up with is that you're grateful for your pet, set a goal around improving your time management skills so you can squeeze in an extra hour with your pet each day. It's the little things that matter most!

To make your new gratitude journaling habit as unintimidating as possible, we have thirty-one spaces where you can jot down small thoughts every day of the month.

You can approach the Yearly Gratitude page one of three ways: 1) noting the big things as they happen; 2) using the circles as free spaces for doodling, journaling, or anything else you can think of; or 3) saving it for your end-of-year reflection.

PRO TIP: . . . .

Pick a time of day to log your gratitude and set a reminder. This will prevent you from forgetting to practice gratitude— or only practicing it when major things happen!

. . . .

MONTH: ....

1. ....

2. ....

3. ....

4. ....

5. ....

6. ....

7. ....

8. ....

9. ....

10. ....

11. ....

12. ....

13. ....

14. ....

15. ....

....

....

....

....

....

....

....

....

....

....

....

....

....

MONTH: ....

1. ....

2. ....

3. ....

4. ....

5. ....

6. ....

7. ....

8. ....

9. ....

10. ....

11. ....

12. ....

13. ....

14. ....

15. ....

....

....

....

....

....

....

....

....

....

....

....

....

....

....

MONTH: ....

1. ....

2. ....

3. ....

4. ....

5. ....

6. ....

7. ....

8. ....

9. ....

10. ....

11. ....

12. ....

13. ....

14. ....

15. ....

....

....

....

....

....

....

....

....

....

....

....

....

....

....

GRATITUDE LOG

MONTH: ....

1. ....

2. ....

3. ....

4. ....

5. ....

6. ....

7. ....

8. ....

9. ....

10. ....

11. ....

12. ....

13. ....

14. ....

15. ....

....

....

....

....

....

....

....

....

....

....

....

....

....

MONTH: ....

1. ....

2. ....

3. ....

4. ....

5. ....

6. ....

7. ....

8. ....

9. ....

10. ....

11. ....

12. ....

13. ....

14. ....

15. ....

GRATITUDE LOG

....

....

....

....

....

....

....

....

....

....

....

....

....

....

MONTH: ....

1. ....

2. ....

3. ....

4. ....

5. ....

6. ....

7. ....

8. ....

9. ....

10. ....

11. ....

12. ....

13. ....

14. ....

15. ....

GRATITUDE LOG

....

....

....

....

....

....

....

....

....

....

....

....

....

....

MONTH: ....

1. ....

2. ....

3. ....

4. ....

5. ....

6. ....

7. ....

8. ....

9. ....

10. ....

11. ....

12. ....

13. ....

14. ....

15. ....

GRATITUDE LOG

MONTH: ....

1. ....

2. ....

3. ....

4. ....

5. ....

6. ....

7. ....

8. ....

9. ....

10. ....

11. ....

12. ....

13. ....

14. ....

15. ....

. ...

. ...

. ...

). ....

. ...

2. ....

3. ....

4. ....

5. ....

6. ....

7. ....

8. ....

9. ....

0. ....

1. ....

GRATITUDE LOG

MONTH: ....

1. ....

2. ....

3. ....

4. ....

5. ....

6. ....

7. ....

8. ....

9. ....

10. ....

11. ....

12. ....

13. ....

14. ....

15. ....

....

....

....

). ....

....

2. ....

3. ....

4. ....

5. ....

6. ....

7. ....

8. ....

9. ....

0. ....

1. ....

MONTH: ....

1. ....

2. ....

3. ....

4. ....

5. ....

6. ....

7. ....

8. ....

9. ....

10. ....

11. ....

12. ....

13. ....

14. ....

15. ....

....

....

....

....

....

....

....

....

....

....

....

....

....

MONTH: ....

1. ....

2. ....

3. ....

4. ....

5. ....

6. ....

7. ....

8. ....

9. ....

10. ....

11. ....

12. ....

13. ....

14. ....

15. ....

GRATITUDE LOG

....

....

....

....

....

....

....

....

....

....

....

....

....

MONTH: ....

1. ....

2. ....

3. ....

4. ....

5. ....

6. ....

7. ....

8. ....

9. ....

10. ....

11. ....

12. ....

13. ....

14. ....

15. ....

....

....

....

....

....

....

....

....

....

....

....

....

....

I'm thankful for...

YEARLY GRATITUDE

CHAPTER 5

TRACK YOUR PROGRESS

f a tree falls in the forest and no one hears it, did it actually make a sound? If you get coffee at a bougie coffee shop and don't Instagram it, did it really happen? If you set a goal and don't measure it, did you really make improvements? The answer to all of these is "yes," but if you're not tracking your progress on your goals, you don't actually have any idea of how much headway you've made.

Lucky for you, we've provided puh-lenty of worksheets for you to measure your progress!

MONTHLY + WEEKLY FOCUS

So far, you've only set yearly goals. The next step is breaking those goals down into monthly and weekly steps. If you stop with your yearly goals, you'll hit what we call the New Year's Resolution Block—you set your goals but you only think of them once a year, when it's time to start over.

To avoid that, you should make time each month, and then each week, to plan out (and check in on) your goals. What are you doing to achieve your goal? What are you focusing on right now? Did you actually accomplish the steps you'd planned to tackle?

In the following worksheets, we've provided space for you to write down which goals you're focusing on each month, as well as the steps you'll take each week to achieve them. As with every other worksheet in this book, feel free to make this space your own so you can choose to focus on just one goal each month, two of them, or all of them.

You know your schedule and lifestyle better than anyone, so it's up to you to decide how much you can take on each week and month. And we'll get to this in a minute, but you can always, always, always revisit the goals you've set and adjust them accordingly.

When you look at the actions you're focusing on to get to your goals, what are they? Are there any that could be considered a habit? After all, when you're forming a habit, you're really just deciding what action you'd like to do every day.

PRO TIP: ●

Notice that we provide space on the Monthly + Weekly Focus pages to write down what you want to accomplish by the end of each month, but not what you did accomplish—we have a dedicated space for reflecting on your achievements in Chapter 6!

● ●

HABIT TRACKING

The habits we form, both good and bad, play a significant role in our lives. Did you know half of the things we do every single day are out of habit?

According to research* by Linnebank et al. comparing the actions that we consciously think about versus those that we complete out of habit, habits are a huge part of our daily lives.

When you set out to form a habit deliberately, whether to support one of the goals you've set or to make a lifestyle change that you think you just need to do, it's not going to be easy. It takes effort, self-discipline, and focus.

One way to support that focus is by tracking your habits. By checking in on a daily basis to hold yourself accountable, you'll build up the habit.

PRO TIP: . . . .

You can also use the habit tracker to break a habit. Whether it's smoking or texting your ex that you want to give up, you'll be able to see how many days you've made it without that bad habit!

. . . .

*Research published as: "Investigating the Balance Between Goal-Directed and Habitual Control in Experimental and Real-Life Settings". Linnebank, F.E., Kindt, M. & de Wit, S. Learn Behav (2018).

For some (particularly competitive) people, streaks contribute to their success. And the longer you work at it, the easier it will be.

Think about it: When you've built up a streak, you'll focus on not missing a day and breaking your perfect score!

How long of a streak do you need?

In 2010, Phillippa Lally, a health psychology researcher at University College London, and her research team designed a study* to learn exactly how long it really takes to form a habit. She found that it takes roughly an average of sixty-six days to form a new habit.

When you pick a habit to work on, make sure you're accounting for it on two months' worth of habit circles. You may find that you need it on even more than that—not everyone forms habits at the same speed, and some habits will take longer to internalize than others. If you're having trouble with your new habit, don't give up!

*Her results were published in the *European Journal of Social Psychology*: "How Are Habits Formed: Modelling Habit Formation in the Real World" if you want to go read the whole thing. Eur. J. Soc. Psychol. 40, 998-1009 (2010).

First, it's worth noting that according to Lally's huge study on habit forming, if you miss one day you're not going to blow the whole thing.

Second, you need to take a look at your life to understand what's keeping you from your goals. There are external factors that could be weighing in. Are you trying to stop biting your nails while you're also handling the busiest season of your job? Or are you swapping thirty minutes of shut-eye for thirty minutes of meditation and ending up sleep-deprived?

Research has also shown that fatigue and stress negatively affect our self-discipline, and in turn, our ability to form habits. If you're really having a hard time waking up twenty minutes earlier, could it be that something's stressing you out and keeping you up at night? If you find yourself ordering takeout more than usual, could it be because you've taken on too much and feel like you don't have the time (or energy) to cook?

According to Lally's research, you're much more likely to stick with a behavior if you do it at the same time every day, or on the same day of each week.

So whether the habit you want to form is drinking a certain amount of water, meal planning for the week, squeezing in a workout, or paying your bills, write it down in your planner or set a recurring alarm on your phone—just try to keep it consistent!

To use the habit tracker circles, pick the habit you'd like to work on and write it next to a circle. Then, every day, go in and color in (or cross out, or doodle on, or something) the space with the corresponding day's number. If it's the first, then color in the box with the 1, the second, 2, and so on and so forth.

PRO TIP: •

We mentioned streaks a few paragraphs ago. If you have a month where you really did stick with your habit every single day, then you can color in the check mark in the middle (or place a giant sticker there, if you're a sticker person). It's a built-in incentive!

• •

Habit suggestions to get you brainstorming (plus room for your own ideas):

Read before bed

···

Take a walk during my lunch break

···

Quit biting my nails

···

···

···

···

···

If all of this stress talk is stressing you out, take a break. Walking for ten minutes, brewing a cup of tea, or even just listening to your favorite song can be a good way to give yourself space to take a breath.

MONTHLY FOCUS

Which goals are you focusing on?

....

....

....

....

WEEKLY FOCUS

	WEEK 1	WEEK 2
Actionable Steps		

ONTH: ....

hat do you want to accomplish by the end of this month?

....

....

....

....

WEEK 3	WEEK 4

INSTRUCTIONS: Write down your habit, then mark the numbered boxes to track your progress.

MONTH: ....

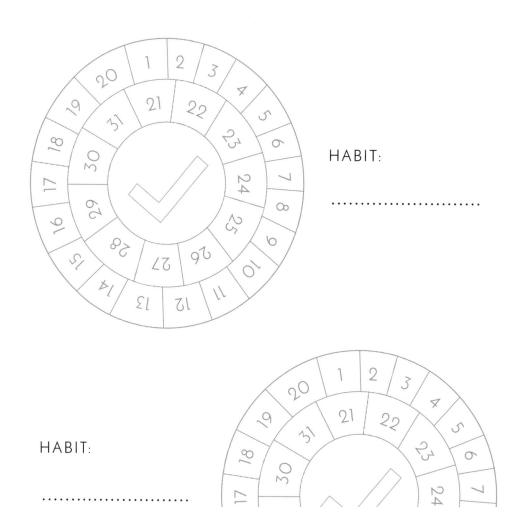

HABIT:

....

HABIT:

....

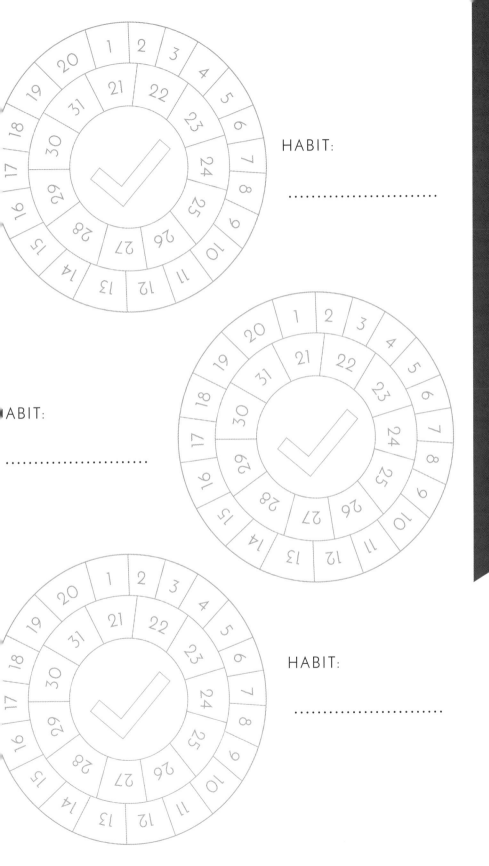

HABIT:

....

ABIT:

....

HABIT:

....

HABIT TRACKER

MONTHLY FOCUS

Which goals are you focusing on?

....

....

....

....

WEEKLY FOCUS

WEEK 1

WEEK 2

Actionable Steps

ONTH: ....

hat do you want to accomplish by the end of this month?

....

....

....

....

WEEK 3

WEEK 4

INSTRUCTIONS: Write down your habit, then mark the numbered boxes to track your progress.

MONTH: ....

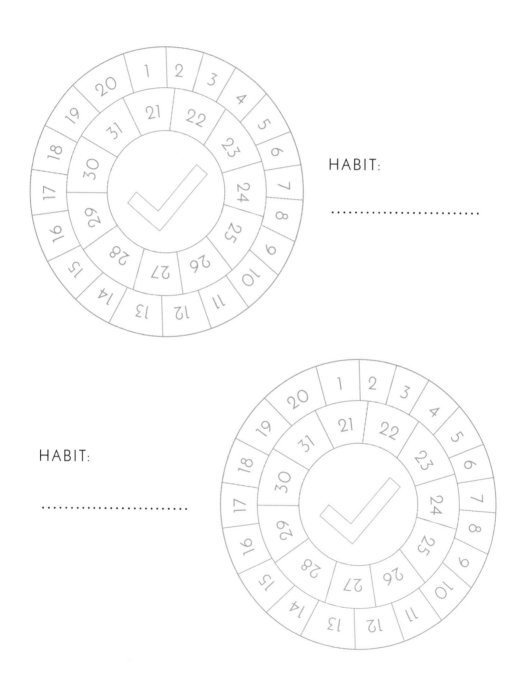

HABIT:

....

HABIT:

....

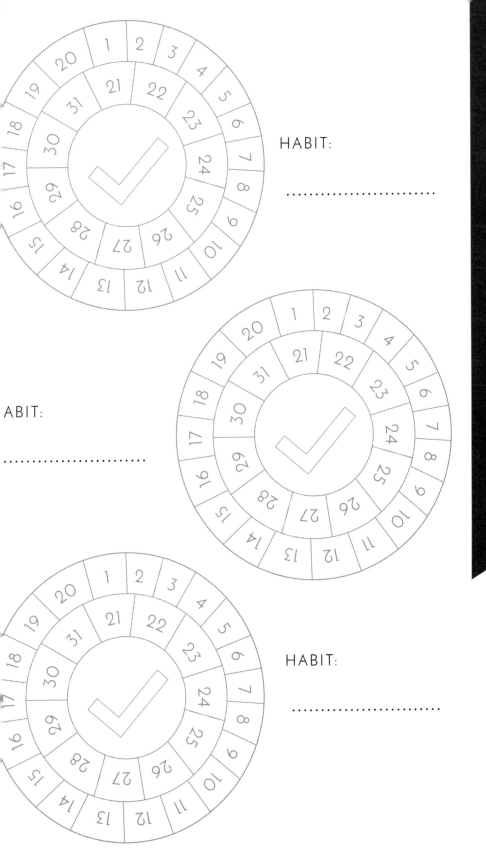

HABIT:

....

ABIT:

....

HABIT:

....

HABIT TRACKER

MONTHLY FOCUS

Which goals are you focusing on?

....

....

....

....

WEEKLY FOCUS

	WEEK 1	WEEK 2
Actionable Steps		

ONTH: ....

hat do you want to accomplish by the end of this month?

....

....

....

....

WEEK 3	WEEK 4

INSTRUCTIONS: Write down your habit, then mark the numbered boxes to track your progress.

MONTH: ....

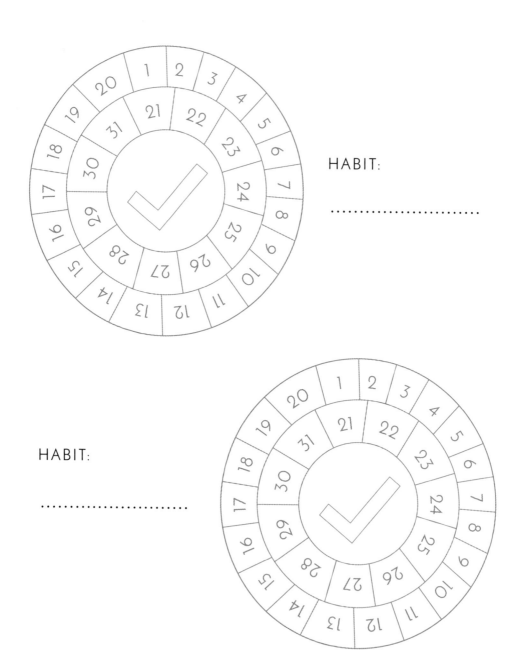

HABIT:

....

HABIT:

....

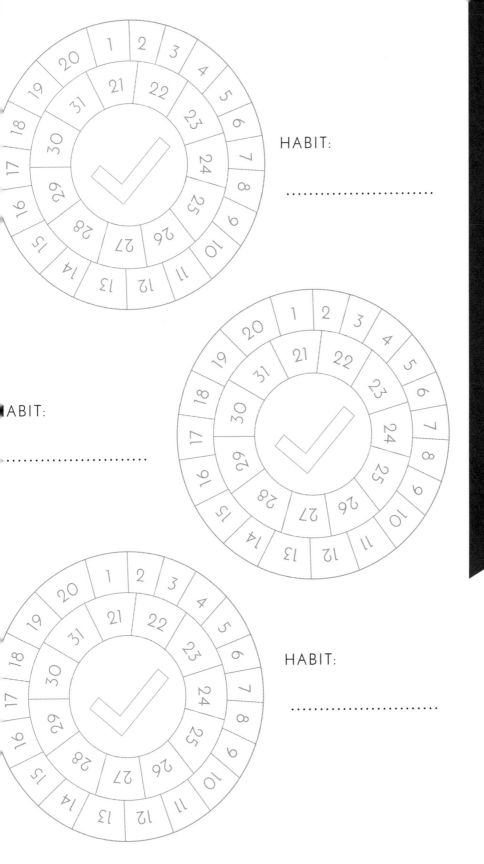

HABIT:

....

ABIT:

....

HABIT:

....

HABIT TRACKER

MONTHLY FOCUS

Which goals are you focusing on?

....

....

....

....

WEEKLY FOCUS

	WEEK 1	WEEK 2
Actionable Steps		

ONTH: ....

hat do you want to accomplish by the end of this month?

....

....

....

....

WEEK 3	WEEK 4

INSTRUCTIONS: Write down your habit, then mark the numbered boxes to track your progress.

MONTH: ....

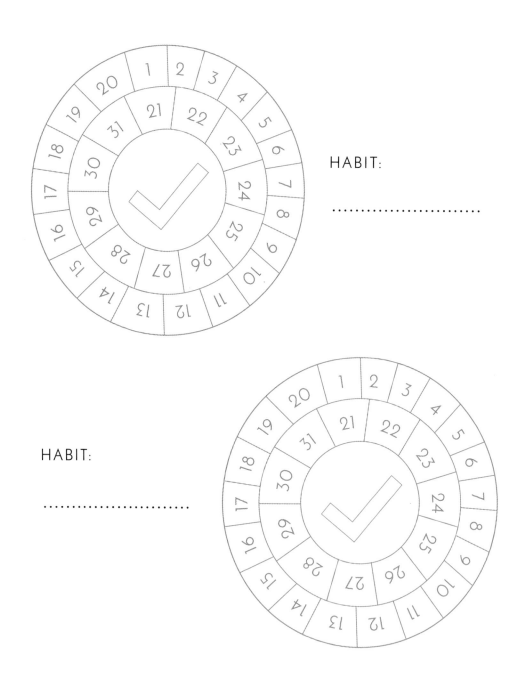

HABIT:

....

HABIT:

....

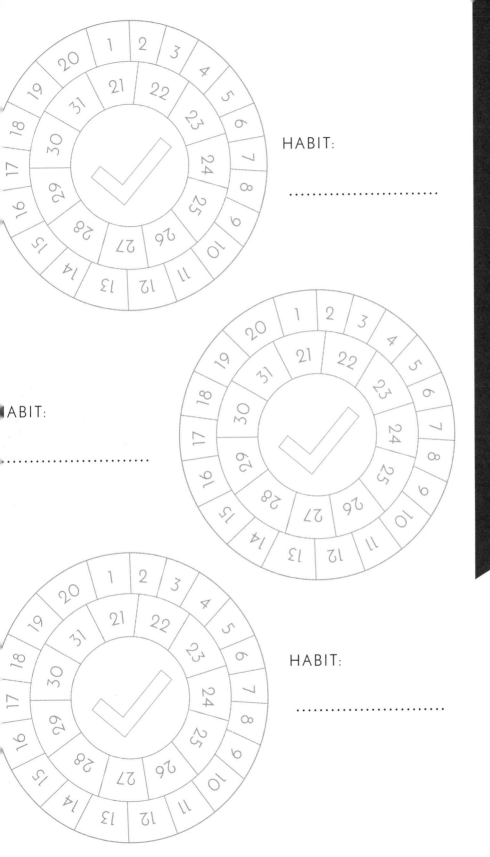

HABIT:

....

ABIT:

....

HABIT:

....

MONTHLY FOCUS

Which goals are you focusing on?

....

....

....

....

WEEKLY FOCUS

	WEEK 1	**WEEK 2**
Actionable Steps		

ONTH: ....

at do you want to accomplish by the end of this month?

....

....

....

....

WEEK 3

WEEK 4

INSTRUCTIONS: Write down your habit, then mark the numbered boxes to track your progress.

MONTH: ....

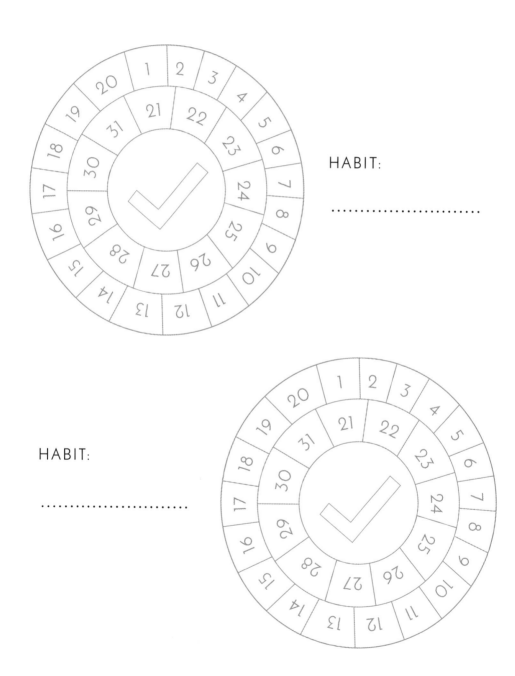

HABIT:

....

HABIT:

....

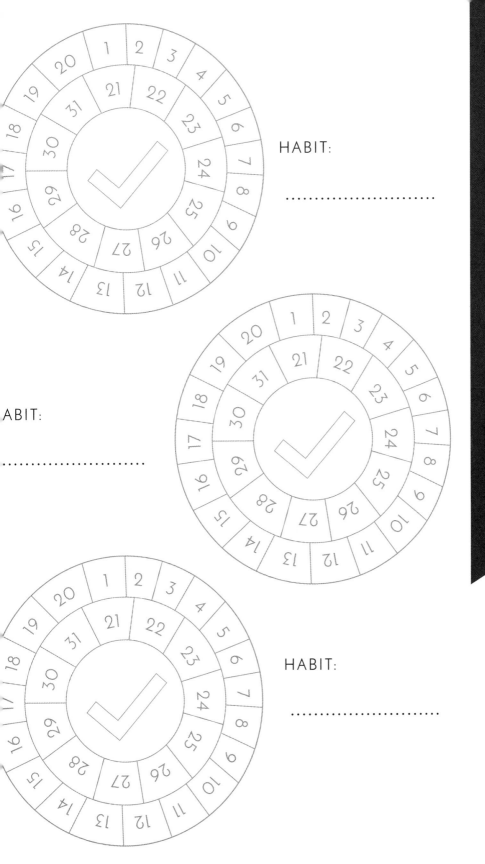

HABIT:

....

ABIT:

....

HABIT:

....

HABIT TRACKER

MONTHLY FOCUS

Which goals are you focusing on?

....

....

....

....

WEEKLY FOCUS

	WEEK 1	WEEK 2
Actionable Steps		

ONTH: ....

at do you want to accomplish by the end of this month?

....
....
....
....

WEEK 3	WEEK 4

INSTRUCTIONS: Write down your habit, then mark the numbered boxes to track your progress.

MONTH: ....

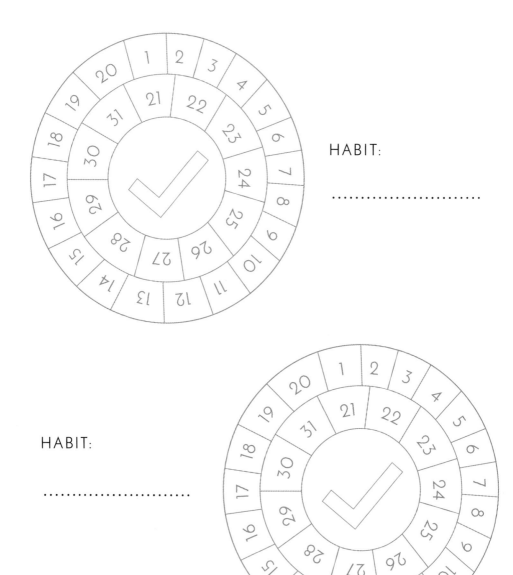

HABIT:

....

HABIT:

....

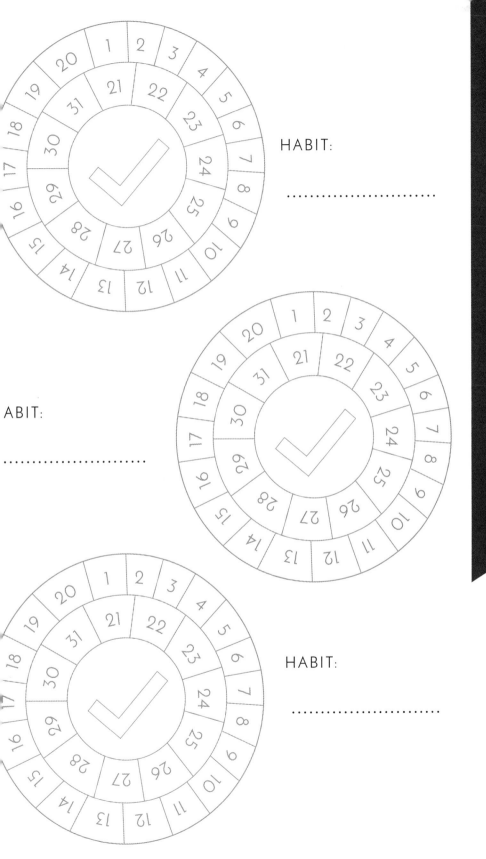

HABIT:

....

ABIT:

....

HABIT:

....

HABIT TRACKER

MONTHLY FOCUS

Which goals are you focusing on?

....

....

....

....

WEEKLY FOCUS

	WEEK 1	WEEK 2
Actionable Steps		

ONTH: ....

hat do you want to accomplish by the end of this month?

....

....

....

....

WEEK 3	WEEK 4

INSTRUCTIONS: Write down your habit, then mark the numbered boxes to track your progress.

MONTH: ....

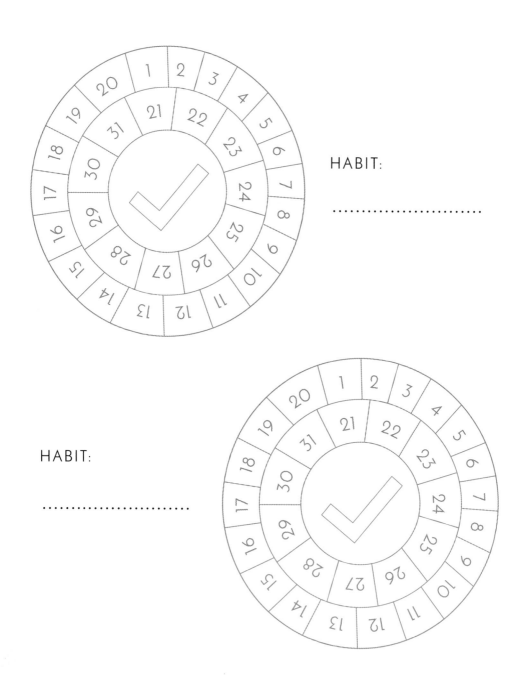

HABIT:

....

HABIT:

....

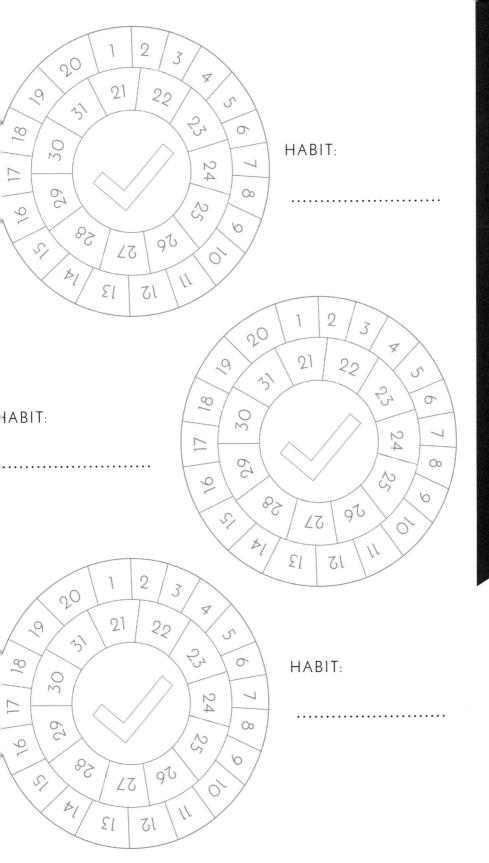

HABIT:

....

HABIT:

....

HABIT:

....

MONTHLY FOCUS

Which goals are you focusing on?

....

....

....

....

WEEKLY FOCUS

	WEEK 1	WEEK 2
Actionable Steps		

ONTH: ....

hat do you want to accomplish by the end of this month?

....

....

....

....

WEEK 3	WEEK 4

INSTRUCTIONS: Write down your habit, then mark the numbered boxes to track your progress.

MONTH: ....

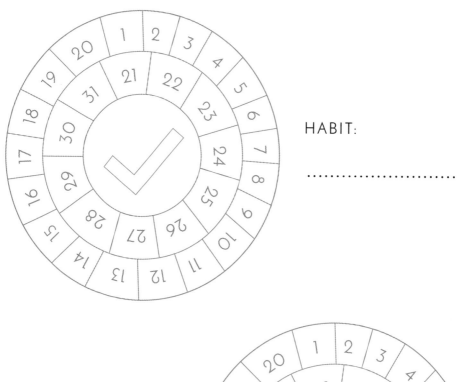

HABIT:

....

HABIT:

....

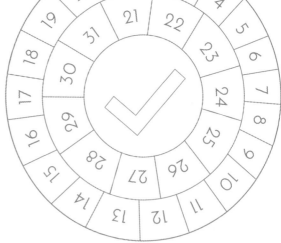

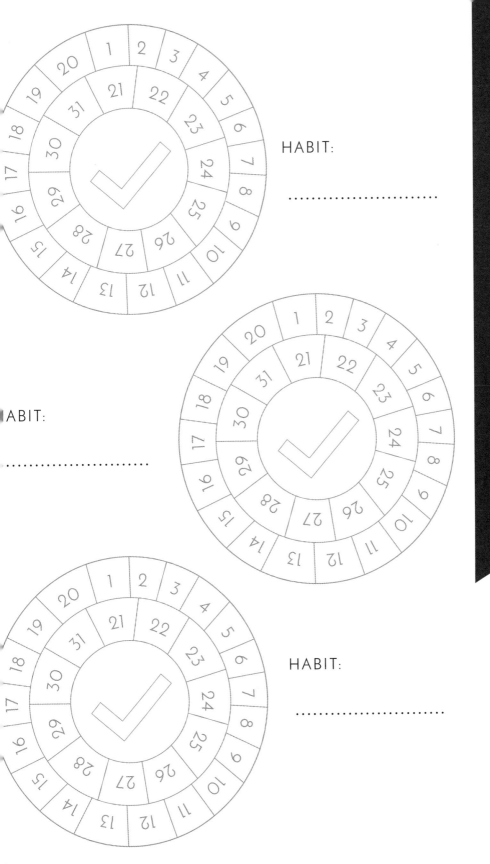

HABIT:

....

ABIT:

....

HABIT:

....

HABIT TRACKER

MONTHLY FOCUS

Which goals are you focusing on?

....

....

....

....

WEEKLY FOCUS

	WEEK 1	WEEK 2
Actionable Steps		

NTH: ....

at do you want to accomplish by the end of this month?

....

....

....

....

WEEK 3　　　　　　　　　WEEK 4

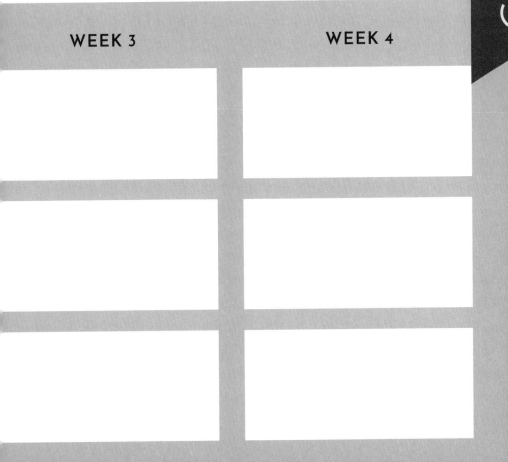

INSTRUCTIONS: Write down your habit, then mark the numbered boxes to track your progress.

MONTH: ....

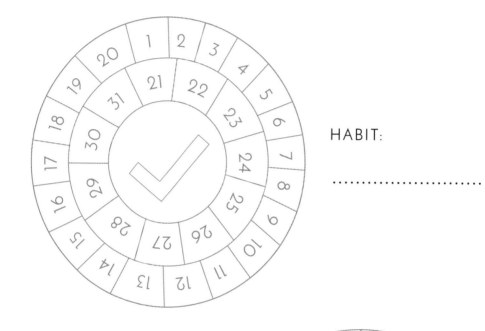

HABIT:

....

HABIT:

....

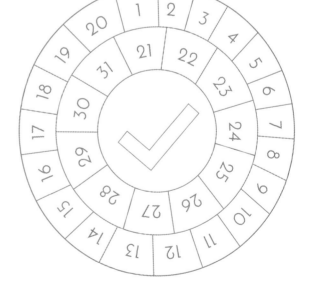

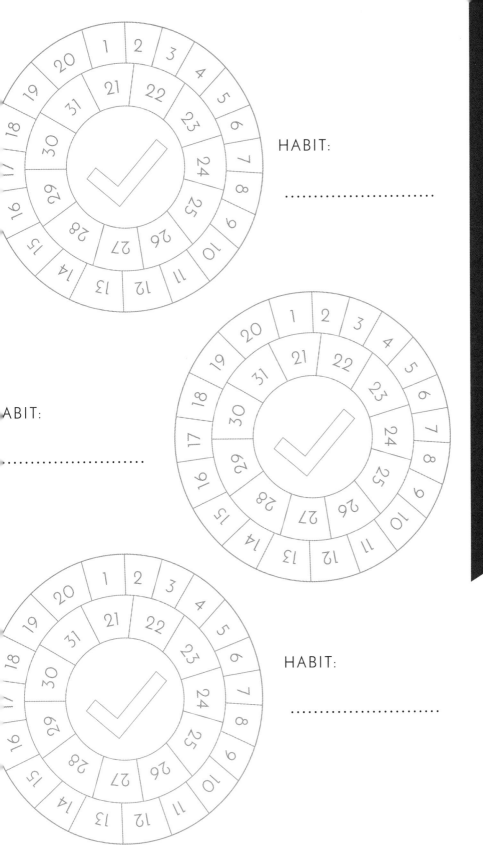

HABIT:

....

ABIT:

....

HABIT:

....

MONTHLY FOCUS

Which goals are you focusing on?

....

....

....

....

WEEKLY FOCUS

	WEEK 1	WEEK 2
Actionable Steps		

ONTH: ....

at do you want to accomplish by the end of this month?

....

....

....

....

WEEK 3	WEEK 4

INSTRUCTIONS: Write down your habit, then mark the numbered boxes to track your progress.

MONTH: ....

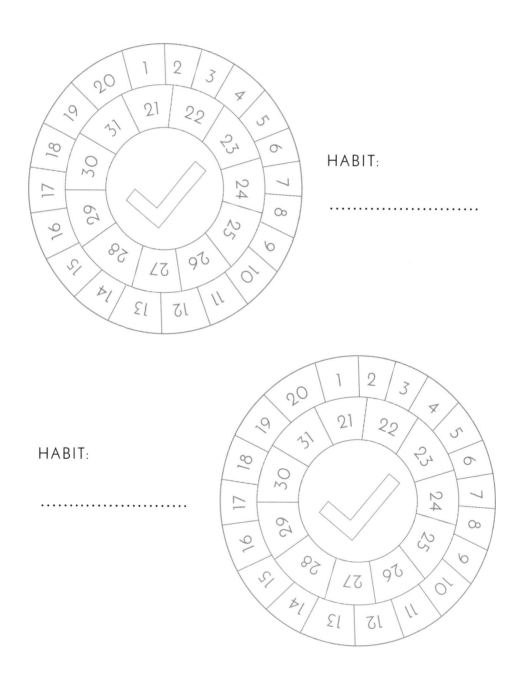

HABIT:

....

HABIT:

....

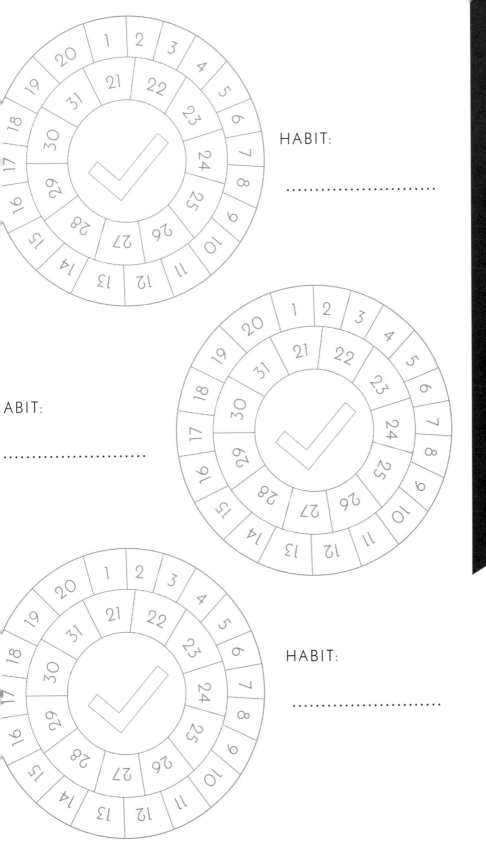

HABIT:

....

ABIT:

....

HABIT:

....

MONTHLY FOCUS

Which goals are you focusing on?

....

....

....

....

WEEKLY FOCUS

	WEEK 1	WEEK 2
Actionable Steps		

ONTH: ....

hat do you want to accomplish by the end of this month?

....

....

....

....

WEEK 3   ## WEEK 4

INSTRUCTIONS: Write down your habit, then mark the numbered boxes to track your progress.

MONTH: ....

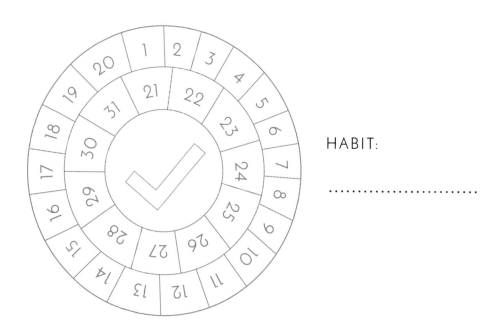

HABIT:

....

HABIT:

....

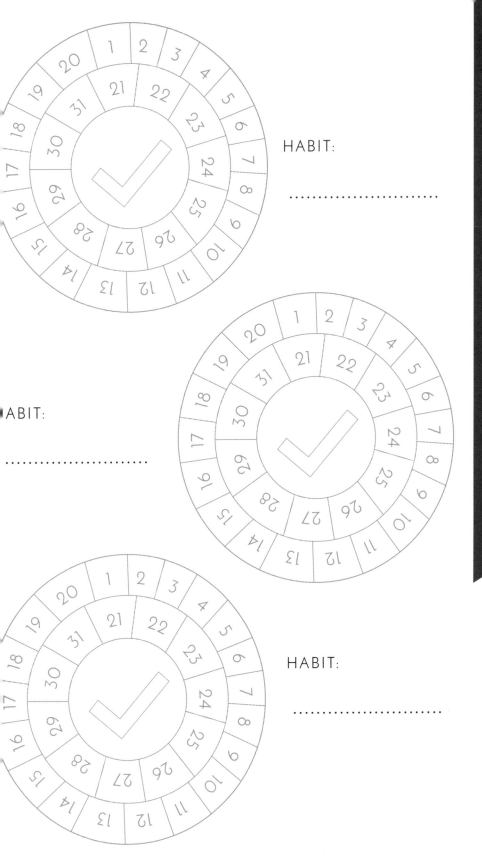

HABIT:

....

ABIT:

....

HABIT:

....

MONTHLY FOCUS

Which goals are you focusing on?

....

....

....

....

WEEKLY FOCUS

	WEEK 1	WEEK 2
Actionable Steps		

ONTH: ....

hat do you want to accomplish by the end of this month?

....

....

....

....

GET FOCUSED

WEEK 3   WEEK 4

INSTRUCTIONS: Write down your habit, then mark the numbered boxes to track your progress.

MONTH: ....

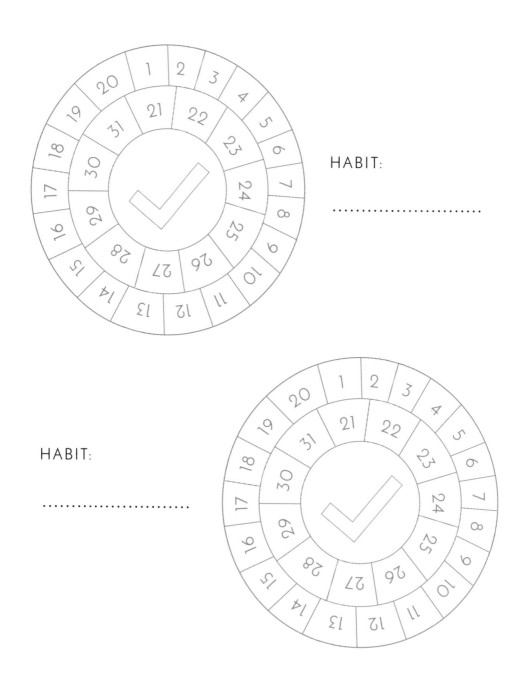

HABIT:

....

HABIT:

....

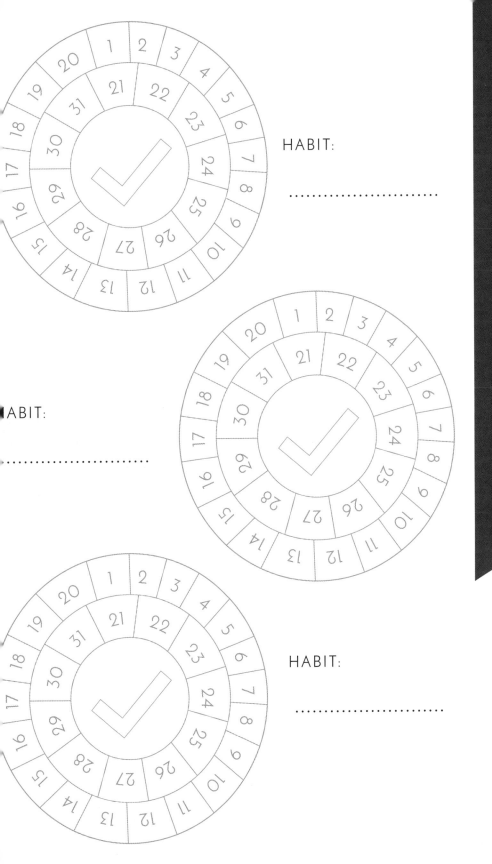

HABIT:

....

ABIT:

....

HABIT:

....

HABIT TRACKER

CHAPTER 6

MIDWAY CHECK-IN

art of being flexible with your goals is recognizing whether or not they're actually working for you. Once you've reached the halfway point on the timeline for your goals (which is completely up to you; it could be two weeks, one month, or even six months), it's important to evaluate your progress (or lack thereof).

When you're halfway through your designated goal timeline, carve some time out of your schedule and answer the questions we've laid out for you on the following worksheets.

If you're way ahead of schedule on your goal, go ahead and raise the bar. If you're not feeling challenged, it can be easy to get bored and fall behind.

Think about it: If you've set a goal to walk one mile every day, after a while that mile becomes easy—and then too easy. Once that mile gets too easy, you wonder "why even take the walk at all?" That's when you should step it up.

For example, you could try to run one mile a day, or walk two miles.

Alternatively, if things are not going well, you need to take some time to regroup. This is absolutely not to say that if something isn't working you should completely ditch your goal.

If you aren't exactly where you thought you would be at this point, you might need to lower the bar a bit or switch up your tactics.

That being said, if it's something you no longer care about, then by all means, go forth and ditch.

For example, if your goal is to walk one mile a day, you could drop that down to half a mile. Or even try walking half a mile twice a day.

PRO TIP: ·

Giving things up cold turkey is a sure-fire way to set yourself up for failure. The key is balance; instead of giving something up or attempting to break a habit completely and all at once, limit yourself. If you're eating pizza once a month instead of once a week, or shopping online once every other month instead of whenever you feel like it, that's progress.

· ·

We've set up a few worksheets to help you with this—they're going to look familiar! To keep things easy, they're a version of the earlier action plan worksheets, but updated especially for a midway check-in.

RE-EVALUATION #1   Goal: ....

Do I still want to achieve this goal? Does it fit my life as it is now? ....

....

....

....

Am I on track for the original deadline for this goal? If not, what's the new

deadline? ....

....

....

....

How has my support system helped me stay on-track with this goal? Should I ask

someone else to help hold me accountable? ....

....

....

Do I have the tools I need to achieve this goal? Do I need more? ....

....

....

tegory: ....

the three actionable steps I set still feel like they will help me

nieve this goal? If not, what other steps can I take? ....

....

....

....

nat steps will I take each week from now on to achieve this goal?

....

....

....

....

nat steps will I take each day from now on to achieve this goal?

....

....

....

....

GOAL RE-EVALUATION

RE-EVALUATION #2   Goal: ....

Do I still want to achieve this goal? Does it fit my life as it is now? ....

....

....

....

Am I on track for the original deadline for this goal? If not, what's the new

deadline? ....

....

....

....

How has my support system helped me stay on-track with this goal? Should I ask

someone else to help hold me accountable? ....

....

....

Do I have the tools I need to achieve this goal? Do I need more? ....

....

....

tegory: ....

the three actionable steps I set still feel like they will help me

hieve this goal? If not, what other steps can I take? ....

....

....

....

hat steps will I take each week from now on to achieve this goal?

....

....

....

hat steps will I take each day from now on to achieve this goal?

....

....

....

....

GOAL RE-EVALUATION

RE-EVALUATION #3

Goal: ....

Do I still want to achieve this goal? Does it fit my life as it is now? ....

....

....

....

Am I on track for the original deadline for this goal? If not, what's the new

deadline? ....

....

....

....

How has my support system helped me stay on-track with this goal? Should I ask

someone else to help hold me accountable? ....

....

....

Do I have the tools I need to achieve this goal? Do I need more? ....

....

....

ategory: ....

the three actionable steps I set still feel like they will help me

hieve this goal? If not, what other steps can I take?   ....

....

....

....

hat steps will I take each week from now on to achieve this goal?

....

....

....

hat steps will I take each day from now on to achieve this goal?

....

....

....

....

GOAL RE-EVALUATION

RE-EVALUATION #4

Goal: ....

Do I still want to achieve this goal? Does it fit my life as it is now? ....

....

....

....

Am I on track for the original deadline for this goal? If not, what's the new

deadline? ....

....

....

....

How has my support system helped me stay on-track with this goal? Should I ask

someone else to help hold me accountable? ....

....

....

Do I have the tools I need to achieve this goal? Do I need more? ....

....

....

ategory: ....

the three actionable steps I set still feel like they will help me

hieve this goal? If not, what other steps can I take? ....

....

....

....

hat steps will I take each week from now on to achieve this goal?

....

....

....

hat steps will I take each day from now on to achieve this goal?

....

....

....

....

GOAL RE-EVALUATION

RE-EVALUATION #5

Goal: ....

Do I still want to achieve this goal? Does it fit my life as it is now? ....

....

....

....

Am I on track for the original deadline for this goal? If not, what's the new

deadline? ....

....

....

....

How has my support system helped me stay on-track with this goal? Should I ask

someone else to help hold me accountable? ....

....

....

Do I have the tools I need to achieve this goal? Do I need more? ....

....

....

Category: ....

Do the three actionable steps I set still feel like they will help me
achieve this goal? If not, what other steps can I take? ....

....

....

....

What steps will I take each week from now on to achieve this goal?

....

....

....

What steps will I take each day from now on to achieve this goal?

....

....

....

....

GOAL RE-EVALUATION

CHAPTER 7

END REFLECTION

his is the final step. If you've reached the end of your timeline, whether you've accomplished your goal 100% or not, it's time to reflect. And once you're done, TREAT. YO'. SELF. And then set some more goals!

Reflections are hard. You've already done the work, right? So what's the point in writing about it? However, this is honestly the step you'll learn the most from. What did and didn't work for you will be invaluable knowledge for you when you set more goals in the future.

You've done a ton of work by this point, so you should take the time to really tally all of that up!

REFLECTION #1

Goal: ....

Did I achieve my goal? If not, what kind of progress did I make? ....

....

....

....

....

....

What helped me stay on track? ....

....

....

....

....

How have I let my support system know I appreciate them? ....

....

....

....

tegory: ....

w can I incorporate the improvements I made to my life in my

tine? ....

....

....

....

at do I want to do with this goal next? ....

....

....

....

w do I feel now that I've completed (or not completed) this goal?'

....

....

....

....

END REFLECTION

REFLECTION #2

Goal: ....

Did I achieve my goal? If not, what kind of progress did I make? ....

....

....

....

....

....

What helped me stay on track? ....

....

....

....

....

How have I let my support system know I appreciate them? ....

....

....

....

tegory: ....

w can I incorporate the improvements I made to my life in my

tine? ....

....

....

....

....

at do I want to do with this goal next? ....

....

....

....

....

w do I feel now that I've completed (or not completed) this goal?

....

....

....

....

REFLECTION #3

Goal: ....

Did I achieve my goal? If not, what kind of progress did I make? ....

....

....

....

....

What helped me stay on track? ....

....

....

....

....

How have I let my support system know I appreciate them? ....

....

....

....

tegory: ....

w can I incorporate the improvements I made to my life in my

tine? ....

....

....

....

....

nat do I want to do with this goal next? ....

....

....

....

....

w do I feel now that I've completed (or not completed) this goal?'

....

....

....

....

REFLECTION #4

Goal: ....

Did I achieve my goal? If not, what kind of progress did I make? ....

....

....

....

....

....

What helped me stay on track? ....

....

....

....

....

How have I let my support system know I appreciate them? ....

....

....

....

tegory: ....

ow can I incorporate the improvements I made to my life in my

utine? ....

....

....

....

....

hat do I want to do with this goal next? ....

....

....

....

....

ow do I feel now that I've completed (or not completed) this goal?'

....

....

....

....

REFLECTION #5

Goal: ....

Did I achieve my goal? If not, what kind of progress did I make? ....

....

....

....

....

....

What helped me stay on track? ....

....

....

....

....

How have I let my support system know I appreciate them? ....

....

....

....

tegory: ....

w can I incorporate the improvements I made to my life in my

utine? ....

....

....

....

....

hat do I want to do with this goal next? ....

....

....

....

....

w do I feel now that I've completed (or not completed) this goal?'

....

....

....

....

CHAPTER 8

PUTTING IT ALL TOGETHER

hether you've only read the book or only filled out the worksheets or you've done both (don't tell the others, but you're our favorite), you've made some MAJOR progress toward achieving your goals.

Before we leave you to go forth and slay your goals, write down three things you learned from this book:

1. ....

2. ....

3. ....

But you're not done yet.

It's not enough to just fill out the worksheets and call it a day; you have to actually put in the work. Here are three things we want you to remember as you work toward accomplishing your goals:

1. Don't lose this book.

You've still got work to do! At this point, you've only barely gotten started. You'll need to check in to track your habits and log the progress you're making toward your goals. You'll have more work to do in six, and then twelve months, and then next year. Plus, even once you're finished with this book, you should refer back to it when creating new goals to see where the bar should be set, which categories still need improvement, and if there are any goals you didn't complete that you want to take another stab at.

PRO TIP: •

Highlight the goals you didn't *quite* achieve, and make a note to try again in the future!

• •

2. Be flexible.

Not every goal you set is going to be the right goal for you for, well, forever. For example, you can control the percent of your income you're moving to savings (a good, measurable goal!), but you could potentially lose your job, leaving you to pull money out of your emergency fund instead.

Maybe you start your goals thinking that you might want to write a novel, but after spending three months honing your creative writing skills, you realize that you're really more interested in magazine writing.

3. Forgive yourself.

Remember—you aren't Wonder Woman! (Or even Diana Prince.) We know, we're sad we aren't, too. That means sometimes you're going to face failure, and that's okay. The important thing is that you learn from your failure, and then you don't let it keep you down.

NOTES, EXTRAS & MORE

 essed up a page and hate the way correction tape looks? Want to get a jumpstart on your next section of goals? We've included some extra worksheets here, as well as some notes pages for random thoughts and tidbits of information.

INSTRUCTIONS: Use this space to brainstorm some goals.

....

....

....

....

....

....

....

....

....

....

....

....

....

....

MONTH: ....

1. ....

2. ....

3. ....

4. ....

5. ....

6. ....

7. ....

8. ....

9. ....

10. ....

11. ....

12. ....

13. ....

14. ....

15. ....

....

....

....

....

....

....

....

....

....

....

....

....

....

I'm thankful for...

YEARLY GRATITUDE

Finances

INSTRUCTIONS:

Sort the goals from your

brain dump (pages 20-21)

into these five categories.

Hobbies

Professional Development

Personal Development

Health + Fitness

SORT IT OUT

MONTHLY FOCUS

Which goals are you focusing on?

....

....

....

....

WEEKLY FOCUS

	WEEK 1	WEEK 2
Actionable Steps		

ONTH: ....

hat do you want to accomplish by the end of this month?

....

....

....

....

WEEK 3	WEEK 4

INSTRUCTIONS: Write down your habit, then mark the numbered boxes to track your progress.

MONTH: ....

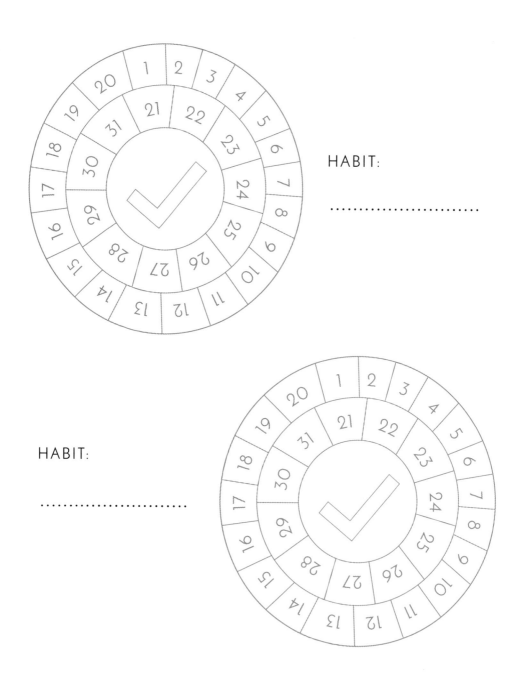

HABIT:

....

HABIT:

....

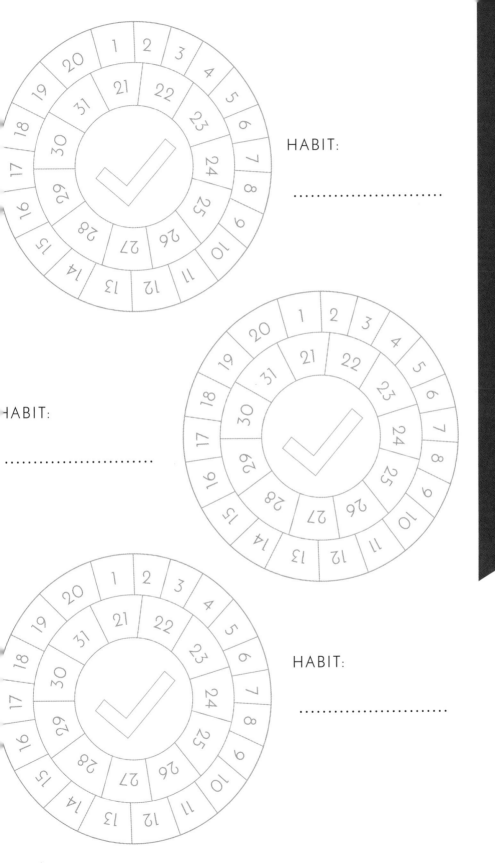

HABIT:

....

HABIT:

....

HABIT:

....

HABIT TRACKER

ELISE WILLIAMS | @melisewilliams

Elise is the Co-Founder and Editor of Earn Spend Live—although when binge-watching *Sailor Moon* and eating frozen pizza becomes a profitable career, she'll leave the world of digital publishing behind. She holds a BA in technical writing from The University of Central Arkansas and resides in Maumelle, AR, with her cat Lazarus.

MELEAH BOWLES | @meleahbowl

Meleah is the other Co-Founder of Earn Spend Live. Usi her feminine wiles and maybe a touch of black magic, s tricked her partner into moving one block away from h mother in Conway, AR with their two dogs and a ferret because why not? She and Elise have known each other f years, but only recently discovered their undyi love for each other. She, too, has a BA in technic writing from The University of Central Arkans